Early English Gardens and Garden Books

By Ellen C. Eyler

PUBLISHED FOR

THE FOLGER SHAKESPEARE LIBRARY

Cornell University Press

THE Elizabethan and Jacobean ages experienced many crises and changes that necessitated new adjustments and sometimes caused a high degree of tension and fear. No householder was too humble to worry about changes in the political order; no man, woman, or child could escape the implications of shifts in economic conditions and disruptions in the traditional pattern of living; nor could anyone forget the haunting danger of recurring plague years. If we in the twentieth century find our conditions of life trying and perplexing, our ancestors who knew the England of Elizabeth I and James I found conditions in their world no less strenuous and troublous. Just as we need release from our tensions, so men and women of the sixteenth and seventeenth centuries required recreations and pleasures that brought them peace and contentment. One source of peaceful pleasure the Elizabethans and Jacobeans found in their gardens. Gardening became for them an activity as characteristically English as afternoon tea and warm beer are today.

"God Almighty first planted a garden," wrote the philosopher Francis Bacon in his essay "Of Gardens" (1625). Bacon continues, in words that are true for all time:

Indeed, it is the purest of human pleasures. It is the greatest refreshment to the spirits of man, without which buildings and palaces are but gross handiworks; and a man shall ever see that when ages grow to civility and elegancy men come to build stately sooner than to garden finely, as if gardening were the greater perfection.

1

Years of turbulence ended when Henry Tudor ascended the shaky throne of England in 1485, and an era of peace and security dawned. No longer necessary were the feudal castles and fortresses that had served as strongholds against civil strife in the Middle Ages. The ending of the Wars of the Roses profoundly influenced domestic living, for in the pacific years following 1485 the Englishman turned his energy to the development of his land and wealth at home and his eyes to the discovery and exploration of new lands and wealth abroad. The parceling-out of the monastic lands after the dissolution of the monasteries under Henry VIII (one-fifth to one-third of the real estate changed hands in one generation) opened an avenue to wealth leading to the building of the fine and stately Tudor and Jacobean mansions, where the garden and house were often designed by the same architect and the garden suggested the quality of living carried on inside. Many of these architects believed with Bacon that landscaping was a difficult but valuable art. John Leland, antiquary and surveyor to King Henry VIII, noted much of this new activity in his travels throughout the countryside, as in the following report from Buckinghamshire:

The old house of the Chenies is so translated by my Lord Russell . . . that little or nothing of it in a manner remaineth untranslated, and a great deal of the house is even newly set up, made of brick and timber, and fair lodgings be new erected in the garden [*The Itinerary of John Leland,* ed. by Thomas Hearne (1710)].

The "fair lodgings" in the garden may have referred to a banqueting house, a popular appurtenance of great houses.

The increased interest in the cultivation of gardens was also influenced by Protestant refugees from the Continent. Huguenots from the Low Countries and France, long skilled in gardening, introduced new vegetables, new flowers, and new methods of cultivation, particularly in East Anglia, where many of them settled. Furthermore, many of the adventurers, mariners, and merchants who sailed away with Elizabeth's blessing

2

and brought a romantic aura to her age returned with roots and seeds from the New and the Old Worlds. In *The Description of England* (1587) William Harrison writes that

strange herbs, plants, and annual fruits are daily brought unto us from the Indies, Americas, Taprobane [Ceylon], Canary Isles, and all parts of the world, . . . and I have seen capers, oranges, and lemons and heard of wild olives growing here, besides other strange trees brought from afar whose names I know not.

Travel on the Continent also increased, and such prominent men as the diplomat Sir Henry Wotton and Baron Zouche of Harringworth brought back from across the Channel new ideas and designs that were of importance in the development of the English garden as we know it.

Literary references in the poetry of Shakespeare and Spenser show the love of flowers and gardens shared by all Englishmen. Members of all classes—country gentlemen, yeomen, house-wives, and simple husbandmen—were laying out their garden plots according to the directions of William Lawson, Thomas Hill, John Parkinson, Gervase Markham, and other authors of that delightful sub-literature, the garden books. Everyone from Queen to cottager loved a garden—as they also desired peace and prosperity—and they lavished much care upon their kitchen gardens, orchards, and the newly emphasized flower gardens.

The English delight in flowers was expressed on most festive occasions. When Elizabeth visited the Earl of Hertford in September, 1591, for instance, she was met by six garlanded girls and led to a miniature crescent-shaped lake, scooped out in honor of Her Majesty's arrival; but en route the royal carriage was stopped by the country people, who showered their sovereign with flowers and gave her nosegays picked from their own yards.

This love of gardens was not new. Two centuries before Elizabeth, Chaucer, a lover of nature above art, gives us a direct and simple but tender expression of love for flowers when he uses the daisy as the emblem of perfect wifehood in *The Legend of Good Women*:

> Now have I thanne eek this condicioun,
> That, of al the floures in the mede,
> Thanne love I most these floures white and rede,
> Swiche as men callen daysyes in our toun.
> To hem have I so gret affeccioun,
> As I seyde erst, whanne comen is the May,
> That in my bed ther daweth me no day
> That I nam up and walkyng in the mede
> To seen this flour ayein the sonne sprede.

In Stephen Hawes's *The History of Grand Amour and la Bell Pucell* (1554) we have a glimpse of the transitional pre-Elizabethan garden:

> Then in we went to the garden glorious,
> Like to a place of pleasure most solacious,
> With Flora painted and wrought curiously,
> In divers knots of marvelous greatness.
> Rampant lions stood up wonderfully,
> Made all of herbs with dulcet sweetness,
> With many dragons of marvelous likeness
> Of divers flowers, made full craftily,
> By Flora colored with colors sundry.
> Amidst the garden so much delectable,
> There was an arbor, fair and quadrant,
> To Paradise right well comparable,
> Set all about with flowers fragrant,
> And in the middle there was resplendishant,
> A dulcet spring and marvelous fountain,
> Of gold and azure, made all certain.

Of the Elizabethans only Shakespeare—more like Chaucer than any other poet in his love of flowers—can describe plants and flowers with such freshness. Henry N. Ellacombe in *The Plant-Lore and Garden-Craft of Shakespeare* (1896) states that the Stratford poet differs largely from Milton and Spenser, who allude chiefly to classical flowers, in that Shakespeare's plants

are thoroughly English plants that (with very few exceptions) he
saw in the hedgerows and woods of Warwickshire or in his own or
his friends' gardens. The descriptions are thus thoroughly fresh
and real; they tell of the country and of the outdoor life he loved,
and they never smell of the study lamp.

When Shakespeare tells us where to find the honeysuckle or,
as it is also called, woodbine, in *Midsummer Night's Dream*
(II.i), we feel that he had a specific spot in mind that he knew
well from his boyhood roamings in the beautiful Warwickshire
countryside.

> I know a bank where the wild thyme blows,
> Where oxlips and the nodding violet grows,
> Quite overcanopied with luscious woodbine,
> With sweet musk roses and with eglantine.

And, certainly, in *The Winter's Tale* (IV.iv) the reader feels
the still warmth of the July or August garden when the poet
writes:

> Here's flowers for you,
> Hot lavender, mints, savory, marjoram;
> The marigold that goes to bed wi' the sun
> And with him rises weeping. These are flowers
> Of middle summer.

In the poetry of Edmund Spenser references to flowers
abound, as in *The Shepherd's Calendar*:

> Bring heather the Pincke and purple Cullambine,
>   with Gelliflowres:
> Bring Coronations and Sops in wine,
>   worne of Paramoures.
> Strowe mee the grounde with Daffadowndillies,
> And Cowslips, and Kingcups, and loued Lillies:
>   The pretie Pawnce,
>   And the Cheuisaunce,
> Shall match with the fayre flowre Delice.

5

Although the orchards, herb gardens, and kitchen gardens had always furnished food for the populace and had been cultivated by Englishmen of all social strata, flower gardening in the sixteenth century developed into a popular art, no longer to be practiced only behind monastic walls and on the grounds of aristocratic residences. The demand for new knowledge of plants and ways of cultivating them furnished the popular press with a market for the garden books written or translated in the period. These books are a joy to read; they are full of common sense and charm, written by men who knew and loved gardening and considered it an important adjunct to their daily life. They wrote of flowers, fruits, and vegetables and they also described methods of watering the garden, fencing it, laying out paths and plots, and caring for bees. Indeed, Englishmen read these books with the same zeal with which they gardened.

The first garden book printed in England was Thomas Hill's *A Most Brief and Pleasant Treatise Teaching How to Dress, Sow, and Set a Garden* (1563). The book proved so popular that it was republished in seven subsequent editions under a new title, *The Profitable Art of Gardening*. Hill was a Londoner, but the London of his time was no metropolitan population center by modern standards; the countryside was not more than two miles away. In *A Survey of London* (1598) John Stow mentions that there were many gardens

wherein are builded many fair summerhouses, . . . with towers, turrets, and chimney tops, not so much for use or profits as for show and pleasure, bewraying the vanity of many men's minds, much unlike to the disposition of the ancient citizens, who delighted in the building of hospitals and almshouses.

With all humility, Hill writes of his "painful pen" and "quaking quill," implying that he is no learned man (though he cites many ancient writers as sources). However this may be, he loved his subject, and his illustrations are valuable for their detail of the small Elizabethan garden and, in a later work, *The Gardener's Labyrinth* (1577), for illustrations of people

6

working in their gardens. This book, in which the author plays on his name and calls himself "Didymus Mountain," was dedicated to Sir William Cecil. Many have criticized Hill for his lack of originality, but we can forgive him when he so sweetly says that the collection of old Continental garden material was "part purchased by friendship and earnest suit of the skillful observers and witty searchers in our time of laudable secrets in garden matters, serving as well for the use and singular comforts of man's life as to a proper gain and delight of the mind."

Another popular book with sections devoted to gardening was Thomas Tusser's *Five Hundred Points of Good Husbandry* (1573), an enlarged edition of *A Hundred Points of Good Husbandry* (1557); the fact that eleven more editions were published by 1600 attests to its popularity. The reader tastes the flavor of life in the small Tudor farmhouse as Tusser, who owned his own farm in the valley of the River Stour, in doggeral diction provides the farmer with directions for his work through the months of the calendar year. One wonders if the master would have sung the following or merely coaxed

Wife, unto thy garden and set me a plot
With strawberry roots of the best to be got.
Such, growing abroad among thorns in the wood,
Well chosen and picked, prove excellent food.

In March, May, and April from morning to night,
In sowing and setting good housewives delight.
To have in a garden or otherlike plot,
To trim up their house and to furnish their pot.

Good peasen and leeks, to make porridge in Lent,
And peasecods in July, save fish to be spent.
Those having, with other things plentiful then,
Thou winnest the heart of the laboring men.

But it is to a Yorkshireman that women owe the first gardening book written solely for them, William Lawson's *The Country Housewife's Garden* (1617). This book was reprinted with his equally popular *A New Orchard and Garden* (1618). Although twentieth-century poet Robert Frost writes "Good fences make good neighbors," three hundred years ago Lawson was advising, "It shall hardly avail you to make any fence for your orchard if you be a niggard of your fruit. For liberality will save it best from noisome neighbors (liberality, I say, is the best fence), as justice must restrain rioters." *A New Orchard and Garden* describes the little gardens that were appearing in increasing numbers as necessary adjuncts of small manor houses and farmhouses; it also characterizes the ideal gardener:

Whosoever desireth and endeavoreth to have a pleasant and profitable orchard must (if he be able) provide himself of a fruiterer, religious, honest, skillful in that faculty, and therewithal painful. . . . The gardener had not need be an idle or lazy lubber, for so your orchard, being a matter of such moment, will not prosper. There will ever be something to do.

Lawson felt that employing a diligent gardener was a practical policy. "The house being served, fallen fruit, superfluity of herbs and flowers, seeds, graffs, sets, and, besides other offal, that fruit which your bountiful hand shall award him withal, will much augment his wages, and the profit of your bees will pay you back again." Recommending work in the orchard and garden as the best type of rest and relaxation, the author says, "For whereas every other pleasure commonly fills some one of our senses, and that only, with delight, this makes all our senses swim in pleasure, and that with infinite variety joined with no less commodity."

In *The Country Housewife's Garden* the author sets forth such general rules as "set moist and sow dry" and "lay no dung to the roots of your herbs as usually they do, for dung not melted is too hot even for trees." As for the novices who might "help," Lawson "adviseth the mistress either to be present herself or to teach her maids to know herbs from weeds." After suggesting that the mistress cultivate herbs and vegetables like rue, pompions (pumpkins), and turnips, he concludes:

I reckon these herbs only because I teach my country housewife, not skillful artists; and it should be an endless labor and would make the matter tedious to reckon up landibeef, stock Julyflower, chervil, valerian, go-to-bed-at-noon, peony, licorice, tansy, garden mints, germander, centaury, and a thousand such physic herbs. Let her first grow cunning in this, and then she may enlarge her garden as her skill and ability increaseth.

While Lawson's books were instructing the simple cottager, his friend Gervase Markham was writing about the orchards and gardens of the Jacobean country house. The versatile Markham wrote on many subjects, from horsemanship and angling to military discipline, and from one of his works on husbandry, *The English Husbandman* (the first part was published in 1613, the second in 1614), we can reconstruct in detail the orchard, pleasure garden, and kitchen garden of the Stuart gentleman. He asserts that the perfect gardener must love his garden and display diligence, application to his appointed tasks, and a knowledge of the art of his craft; he scoffs at gardens that can be easily cultivated, as in the south of England, and praises the hard-labored beauties of gardens made on dry, barren ground, as on moors or hills. Markham claims to be a true English husbandman and will not try to emulate the ways of France, Italy, or Germany. "Yet I, that am all English husbandman and know our soils out of the worthiness of their own natures, do as it were rebel against foreign imitation, thinking their own virtues are able to propound their own rules." Englishmen might modify the new ideas about gardens brought over from the Continent, but, as the above statement implies, the gardens were to be strictly English. Another book by Markham, *The English Housewife* (1631), provides the mistress with rules for planting, along with other necessary material on country-house management.

Two books treating single themes appeared in the first decade of the seventeenth century. In 1603 Richard Gardiner's *Profitable Instructions for Manuring, Sowing, and Planting of Kitchen Gardens* was published. This book by a Shrewsbury linen draper was the first to center entirely on vegetable growing. Curiously, however, Gardiner never mentioned the potato. Although potatoes were certainly known in England by this time, other vegetables in Shropshire were regarded as more important. One N. F. wrote *The Husbandman's Fruitful Orchard* (1608), a book containing useful instructions on how to gather and preserve fruit.

Sir Hugh Plat, who in 1594 had published a collection of Latin *sententiae*, subsequently turned his attention to food production and food preservation—both of which were important to the Elizabethan, whose farming methods were still relatively unimproved. He knew that food must be preserved until the next harvest, which in the end might fail. Plat wrote several discourses on manuring and sowing of grain and then a book on gardening, *Floraes Paradise* (1608), which under a later title, *The Garden of Eden* (1653), was to be read avidly by many a seventeenth-century gardener. One is aware of the age of Bacon when Plat says in his epistle to the reader that in the two hundred experiments set forth in the book

I bring substantial and approved matter with me, though I leave method at this time to schoolmen, who have already written many large and methodical volumes of this subject (whose labors have greatly furnished our studies and libraries but little or nothing altered or graced our gardens and orchards).

He wrote an earlier book on the stillroom, "a most important adjunct" of the garden, entitled *Delights for Ladies to Adorn Their Persons, Tables, Closets, and Distillatories* (1602). The chapter headings well describe the book's contents: "The Art of Preserving, Conserving, Candying, etc.," "Secrets in Distillation," "Cookery and Housewifery," and "Sweet Powders, Ointments, Beauties, etc." With simple faith, the wives of noblemen, yeomen, and squires practiced the economy of *Delights for Ladies* in their country homes. Plat's directions include such items as how to keep "clusters of grapes" till Easter and how "to preserve oranges after the Portugal fashion." Certainly the volume's charming epistle "to all true lovers of art and knowledge" captures the spirit and quiet beauty of homely life in the country.

Let piercing bullets turn to sugar balls;
The Spanish fear is hushed and all their rage.
Of marmalade and paste of Genoa,
Of musked sugar, I intend to write,
Of leach, of sucket, and quiddany, [jellies and preserved fruit]
Affording to each lady her delight.
I teach both fruits and flowers to preserve,
And candy them, so nutmegs, cloves, and mace;
To make both marchpane paste and sugared plate,
And cast the same in forms of sweetest grace,
Each bird and fowl so molded from the life,
And after cast in sweet compounds of art,
As if the flesh and form which Nature gave
Did still remain in every limb and part.
When crystal frosts have nipped the tender grape,
And clean consumed the fruits of every vine,
Yet here behold the clusters fresh and fair,
Fed from the branch or hanging on the line.
The walnut, small nut, and the chestnut sweet,
Whose sugared kernels lose their pleasing taste,
Are here from year to year preserved meet,
And made by art with strongest fruits to last.
The artichoke and the apple of such strength,
The quince, the pomegranate, with the barberry,
No sugar used, yet color, taste, and smell,
Are here maintained and kept most naturally.

Undoubtedly the favorite garden book of the early seventeenth century, particularly of the owners of the spacious gardens, was John Parkinson's *Paradisi in sole, Paradisus terrestris* (1629), dedicated to Queen Henrietta Maria. In simple but beautiful prose the author, who had been apothecary to King James, describes his "speaking garden" or garden of pleasant flowers, his kitchen garden, and his orchard. His pride

11

in each individual flower can be sensed in this passage on the daffodil: "I think none ever had this kind before myself, nor did I myself ever see it before the year 1618, for it is of mine own raising and flowering first in my garden." The following paragraph from the preface sets the tone of the book:

For, truly, from all sorts of herbs and flowers we may draw matter at all times, not only to magnify the Creator (that hath given them such diversities of forms, scents, and colors that the most cunning workman cannot imitate and such virtues and properties that although we know many yet many more lie hidden and unknown), but many good instructions also to ourselves; that, as many herbs and flowers with their fragrant sweet smells do comfort and, as it were, revive the spirits and perfume a whole house, even so such men as live virtuously, laboring to do good and profit the Church of God and the commonwealth by their pains or pen, do, as it were, send forth a pleasant savor of sweet instructions, not only to that time wherein they live and are fresh, but being dry, withered, and dead, cease not in all after ages to do as much or more.

At the same time that Englishmen were writing books on these subjects, many foreign works were being translated for the English public. Even though many ideas and customs of Renaissance Italy were being adopted during this period, no Italian gardening books were translated, perhaps because Italian styles were too elaborate for most English gardeners. Ordinary folk found translations from Dutch and French writers more valuable. Two of the most popular were the minor poet Barnabe Googe's translation of *Four Books of Husbandry* (1577), by the Dutch writer Conrad Heresbach, and Richard Surflet's translation from the French of *Maison Rustique; or, The Country Farm* (1600), written by Charles Estienne and his son-in-law Jean Liebault. Heresbach employs a dramatic form and a cast of four, including Marius, the host, and Thrasybulus, the guest from court. While walking about the garden and orchard, Marius explains to his friend why he lives in the country, how much the house should cost, and how the daily routine should be carried out. Although Italian ideas may have been too grand for modest English homes, some of the features of French gardens described in *Maison Rustique*—arbors, fountains, mazes, streams of water, and great alleys between the kitchen gardens and pleasure gardens—were adopted by English householders.

Many Englishmen also owned copies of the botanical works of the sixteenth and early seventeenth centuries. William Turner, the father of English botany, John Gerard, and John Parkinson were categorizing plants according to the botanical classifications of the time and giving suggestions as to their use. For example, Turner's *A New Herbal* (published in three parts, 1551, 1562, and 1568) contains words of caution against the excessive use of herbs like the onion: "Onions eaten in meat largely make the head ache; . . . they make them forgetful which in the time of their sickness use them out of measure." Like other Elizabethans, Turner was a man of many worlds, for he was a divine, a physician, and a botanist. Twentieth-century psychiatrists would find altogether too simple John Gerard's cure for the nightmare. In his *Herbal* (1597) the gardener to William Cecil recommends this remedy under the heading "peony": "The black grains (that is the seed) to the number of fifteen, taken in wine or mead, is a special remedy for those that are troubled in the night with the disease called ephialtes or nightmare, which is as though a heavy burden were laid upon them and they oppressed therewith." Gerard alludes throughout to contemporary life, his friends, and his own experiences with flowers. Salads today are not so imaginative as in the sixteenth century, when Gerard wrote: "Those of our time do use the flowers in salads to exhilarate and make the mind glad. There be also many things made of them, used everywhere for the comfort of the heart, for the driving away of sorrow and increasing the joy of the mind."

Parkinson's *Theatrum botanicum* (1640) contains many curious pieces of information, along with descriptions of some 3,800 plants. He tells the country housewife to use the common weed horsetail to scour her wooden, pewter, and brass vessels and to boil the young tops of the same weed and eat them like asparagus. For an unwelcome guest he prescribes a bitter salad of cuckoopint root, chopped and tossed with endive or lettuce. The evolution in gardening, as in all the arts, was slow. During the reigns of Henry VII and Henry VIII features of the feudal period were still obvious. Moats and battlements existed, but they now served to protect the garden from marauding neighbors and rabbits. By the time of Elizabeth the medieval atmosphere had all but disappeared. When men searched for sites for their comfortable manor houses, they chose places with views, perhaps on a hill or by a river, instead of selecting hills to be fortified. One requirement of the new age was a suitable location for a garden.

Nevertheless, Tusser in 1575 does not mention the flower garden. Lawson in 1617 explains the need for two gardens, giving reasons both practical and aesthetic:

Herbs are of two sorts, and therefore it is meet (they requiring divers manners of husbandry) that we have two gardens—a garden for flowers and a kitchen garden, or a summer garden and a winter garden. Not that we mean so perfect a distinction that the garden for flowers should or can be without herbs good for the kitchen, or the kitchen garden should want flowers, nor on the contrary; but for the most part they would be severed. First, because your garden flowers shall suffer some disgrace if among them you intermingle onions, parsnips, etc. Secondly, your garden that is durable must be of one form, but that which is for your kitchen's use must yield daily roots or other herbs and suffer deformity. Thirdly, the herbs of both will not be both alike ready at one time either for gathering or removing.

In 1629, however, Parkinson is appealing solely to man's aesthetic sense when he discusses separate gardens:

As before I showed you that the beauty of any worthy house is much the more commended for the pleasant situation of the garden of flowers or of pleasure to be in the sight and full prospect of all the chief and choicest rooms of the house, so, contrariwise, your herb garden should be on the one or other side of the house and those best and choice rooms. For the many different scents that arise from the herbs, as cabbages, onions, etc., are scarce well pleasing to perfume the lodgings of any house; and the many overtures and breaches, as it were, of many of the beds thereof, which must necessarily be, are also as little pleasant to the sight.

The vegetable garden was moved from the front of the house, and flowers assumed new roles for even the simple cottager. But, as Lawson writes, there was not "so perfect a distinction," for flowering herbs bordered the knots in the flower gardens and lime (linden) trees shaded the garden alleys. One garden, containing flowering fruit trees, typical English flowers, herbs, and vegetables, served the lesser gentry and yeomen.

"Peregrination charms our senses with such unspeakable and sweet variety," wrote Robert Burton in *The Anatomy of Melancholy* (1621). Indeed, English travelers, having seen the Italian gardens designed by men like San Gallo and Raphael, probably brought back ideas from which originated the fountains, statues, vases, and terraces that were prevalent in sixteenth-century English gardens. But the classicism of such Italian gardens was more at home in Jacobean days, for the intricate designs characteristic of Renaissance art became quite fanciful in the imaginative minds of Tudor Englishmen. The English pleasure garden called to mind the England of Puck and the fairies, a happy England of pageantry and gaiety, of men and women enjoying gardens where fantastic fountains surprised ladies with sudden showers, where people walked in garden alleys and played in mazes, fished from the tops of mounts, and made love in the arbors, an England where the Queen herself entertained ambassadors in her Whitehall gardens. At Kenilworth "the people, . . . the fruit trees, the plants, the herbs, the flowers, the change in colors, the birds flittering, the fountain streaming, the fish swimming, all in such delectable variety," were reminiscent of Paradise, wrote Robert Laneham to Humphrey Martin, a London mercer, in *A Letter*

Wherein Part of the Entertainment unto the Queen's Majesty at Killingworth Castle . . . Is Signified (1575).

The most important feature of the pleasure ground was the enclosed garden, sometimes a succession of small enclosures, which prompted Sir Henry Wotton to exclaim that upon approaching each new terrace he felt as if he were being magically transplanted to a new garden. Mazes, mounts, knot beds or other flowering plots, statues, fountains, sundials, obelisks, shaded alleys, turfed seats, carved wooden figures, and works of topiary were commonplace. Whereas banqueting houses and marble statues were found in the gardens of the wealthy, commoners built trellised arbors and clipped trees to form figures. One had a sense of space only on the bowling green or tennis court beyond—the only turfed areas.

The gardens were thus full of activity and greatly enhanced the enjoyment of Tudor and Jacobean home life. In developing their own national style, the English had blended native and foreign elements to suit their climate and their own personalities. Practicality was never abandoned, but more thought was given to beauty and harmony than in the gardens of Chaucer's day.

The flower garden was usually planted on the south side of the house, which enabled it to get the full benefit of the sun and the protection the house afforded from the north winds. Markham advocated such a plan, recommending that the chief rooms have the view of the garden, while the kitchen and buttery received the advantage of the cooler northern exposure. People were cautious about planting too close to odorous sloughs or near barns, where chaff from the grain might blow onto the garden.

The formal English flower garden was not carelessly conceived but was based on the eastern four-plot design brought back to western Europe by the Crusaders. The manor house occupied the center of the design, with a forecourt leading to its entrance. On the service side of the house was the kitchen garden, on the third side the orchard, and on the back side, faced by the chief rooms, lay the ornamental garden. There also the four-plot plan was used. Walks crossed the garden, cutting out rectilineal forms, and upon viewing these symmetrically balanced squares and rectangles from the raised terrace alongside the house one could see a resemblance to a Persian carpet. A predominant feature of Tudor architecture was the use of horizontal lines intercepted by perpendicular ones in the geometric tracery atop the house. The same design was often the pattern for the knots and mazes, while the forthrights, or garden paths, paralleled the house plan. Parkinson recommends this harmonious four-plot plan in *Paradisi in sole*:

The foursquare form is the most usually accepted with all and doth best agree to any man's dwelling. . . . Yet if it be longer than the breadth or broader than the length the proportion of walks, squares, and knots may be soon brought to the square form and be so cast as the beauty thereof may be no less than the foursquare proportion, or any other better form, if any be. To form it, therefore, with walks, cross the middle both ways and round about it also with hedges, with squares, knots, and trails, or any other work within the four square parts, is according as every man's conceit alloweth of it and they will be at the charge.

Evidence exists that terraced areas were commonly used. At Drayton, an Elizabethan house in Northamptonshire, there is not only a terrace in front of the house but also a wide one along the outer wall of the garden. There are descriptions of terraces at Kenilworth and at Wilton, the Earl of Pembroke's estate. Flights of steps connected the terrace with the garden walks and the garden levels with each other. The terrace adjoining the house was anywhere from three to ten feet above the garden; its area depended on the size of the house and the contour of the land. The ground was either turfed or graveled, and often flower beds were planted. A view from the terrace edge, protected by stone balustrades or openwork, would exemplify the garden-within-a-garden concept loved by the Elizabethans and illustrated by Plate 3 from *A New Orchard and Garden*. Here are six enclosed gardens on three levels. The terrace nearest the house contains a square planted with fruit trees, with flower beds among the trees and in the border, and another square suggesting topiary work—a man with a drawn sword and a prancing horse. On the middle level is a knot garden, shaped like a Yorkist rose with a six-pointed star, and another fruit garden. Two kitchen gardens are on the lowest level. Markham discusses a similar plan in *The English Husbandman*:

And herein you shall understand that there be two forms of proportions belonging to the garden, the first only beautiful, as the plain and single square, containing only four quarters with his large alleys every way; . . . the other both beautiful and stately, as when there is one, two, or three leveled squares, each mounting seven or eight steps one above another, and every square containing four several quarters with their distinct and several alleys of equal breadth and proportion. . . . And herein I would have you understand that I would not have you to cast every square into one form or fashion of quarters or alleys, for that would show little variety or invention in art, but rather to cast one in plain squares, another in triangulars, another in roundels, and so a fourth according to the worthiness of conceit, as in some sort you may behold by these figures, which, questionless, when they are adorned with their ornaments, will breed infinite delight to the beholders.

The gardener strove for an impenetrable outer enclosure, for the proximity of woodland meant that the enemies to be kept out were goats, sheep, hares, rabbits, cattle, and horses. Quickset hedges, planted in privet or whitethorn, were quite popular, yew being employed to shade the garden alleys and box to border the flower beds. Thomas Hill claimed that whitethorn "waxeth so thick and strong that hardly any person can enter into the ground saving by the garden door." Bacon's description of his desired hedge is amusing. He who called knots "toys" and disdained topiary work as being "for children" described a most ambitious plan:

The garden is best to be square, encompassed on all the four sides with a stately arched hedge. The arches to be upon pillars of carpenter's work of some ten foot high and six foot broad, and the spaces between of the same dimension with the breadth of the arch. Over the arches let there be an entire hedge of some four foot high, framed also upon carpenter's work, and upon the upper hedge, over every arch, a little turret, with a belly, enough to receive a cage of birds, and over every space between the arches some other little figure, with broad plates of round, colored glass gilt for the sun to play upon. But this hedge I intend to be raised upon a bank, not steep but gently slope[d], of some six foot, set all with flowers.

Lawson would combine a hedge with a moat, the advantages of the moat being that it would "afford you fish, fence, and moisture to your trees, and pleasure also. . . . You may have swans and other water birds, good for devouring of vermin, and a boat for many good uses." Walls of brick or stone were common, with flowers like rosemary blooming along them. In *Measure for Measure* (IV.i) Isabella tells the Duke, "He hath a garden circummured with brick." Markham mentions an earthen wall planted with wallflowers.

Generally the garden's main entrance was a wrought iron gate. Smaller wooden doors (Isabella speaks of a "planched gate" and "a little door" from the vineyard to the garden) opened onto the orchard and kitchen garden. If not of wrought iron, the gate was built of stone to form piers and arches, ornamented by obelisks, balls, and heraldic beasts. A gatehouse flanked the more elaborate entrance.

In the medieval monastic gardens so-called mounts were erected; these were artificial hills of earth that could be surmounted by steps or a winding path. From the top, monks peered over their monastery walls at the world beyond. Mounts were also found in the sixteenth-century garden, and Bacon believed that they should be crowned by a banqueting house and be treated as the central feature of a "princelike garden." The more practical Lawson thought that atop a mount one had a good position from which to shoot a buck or fish in the stream that ideally would flow below the garden wall. He would cover his mount "with fruit trees, Kentish cherries, damsons, plums, etc., with stairs of precious workmanship, and in some corner (or mo) a true dial or clock and some antic works; and especially silver-sounding music, mixed instruments, and voices gracing all the rest."

The layout of the paths and alleys was stressed, for not only were they daily traversed by the garden-loving occupants but also they lent form to the garden. The German traveler Paul Hentzner wrote that following every meal at Oxford there was free time for a stroll in the garden, and Elizabeth too took such brisk morning exercise at Nonsuch and Whitehall. In the stately gardens the broad alleys, or forthrights, surrounded the pleasure garden and gave it a general design, while narrower paths intersected between the garden beds. Parkinson pointed out that "the fairer and larger your alleys and walks be, the more grace your garden shall have, the less harm the herbs and flowers shall receive by passing by them that grow next unto the alley's sides, and the better shall your weeders cleanse both the beds and the alleys." Few walks were turfed; more often they were sanded, graveled, or planted with the sweet-smelling herbs suggested by Bacon: "Those which perfume the air most delightfully, not passed by as the rest but being trodden upon and crushed, are three, that is, burnet, wild thyme, and water mints; therefore you are to set whole alleys of them to have the pleasure when you walk or tread." Camomile was also planted. The narrow paths between the beds were sanded, for when walking on dewy grass, Markham sagely observes, "shoes or boots of extraordinary goodness" must be worn. Often sand was mixed with pebbles and coal dust, a recommended weed killer. A low-growing hedge of lavender, box, rosemary, sage, or lavender cotton bordered these narrow paths.

Wider paths became open alleys, pleached bowers, or arbors ("herbers," as Hill called them). High, clipped hedges were planted in cypress, privet, thorn, fruit trees, roses, briers, juniper, hornbeam, cornel, and pyracantha—gay with its red berries during the winter months. For these alleys Parkinson would plant sweetbrier, whitethorn, privet, and roses, which could be enlaced along the hedge. Pleached bowers were formed of trees that branched overhead and entwined. The willow, lime, wych-elm, hornbeam, privet, whitethorn, and maple shaded these "covert" walks, with sweetbriers, honeysuckles, roses, and rosemary planted here and there. The arbors might be built along the enclosure wall, with fragrant climbers of rosemary, jasmine, or musk roses spread over their wooden latticework. Windows were fashioned in an arbor of considerable length, enabling one to view the garden from different points. A similar structure or a more sturdy wooden gallery connected the house with the chapel or other buildings on the property.

Along these walks and at terminal points the stroller might discover spots to rest—perhaps even a banqueting house in the huge formal gardens of great estates. In small gardens one might find seats placed in the recesses of the wall or hedge or under an arbor, where grew roses, clematis, or honeysuckles. Wild vines, hops, jasmine, gourds, cucumbers, runner beans, and sweetbrier also climbed this small edifice. Near its entrance clipped cypress, cedar, and box trees stood. Arbors with round-turreted roofs—resembling a colonial New England summer-house—often graced a mount or were erected in the garden corners.

With that ebullient spirit characteristic of Elizabeth's England, men and women planted flower beds composed of clusters of blossoms, anticipating Parkinson's wish that the garden appear "like a piece of tapestry of many glorious colors to increase everyone's delight." Flowers also grew under trees in the orchards or along the garden walks, but Bacon cautioned that such planting be done "thin and sparingly, lest they deceive the trees," and the usual practice was to plant in open beds or open knots rather than in the more complicated knot patterns. Parkinson preferred the open beds because he felt that there was no room in the interstices of the knots for other flowers. If raised above the level of the path, as was done in the Middle Ages, the bed was supported by oak boards, tiles, lead, or the shank bones of sheep. An edging of jawbones, used in the Low Countries, Parkinson called "too gross and base." Lawson implied that many gardeners did not know why they raised their beds: "The garden's soil would be somewhat drier, because herbs, being more tender than trees, can neither abide moisture nor drought in such excessive measure as trees, . . . and this is the cause (if they know it) that gardeners raise their squares." A railed wooden fence, often painted, surrounded these plots.

Although the authors of the garden literature favored the open beds for their flowers, their volumes usually included plans for the closed or knotted beds. In geometric or abstract designs, such patterns were outlined in low, close-growing plants like hyssop, germander, marjoram, savory, thrift, thyme, juniper, yew, dwarf box, and lavender cotton. Markham speaks of elaborate knots forming coats of arms in the gardens of noblemen and simple knots on which linen dried in the country housewife's garden. French or Dutch box or lavender cotton bordered these beds and spring flowers—daffodils, primroses, and hyacinths—grew in the open spaces of the patterns. The practice of covering this area with different-colored sands was admonished by Bacon, for "you may see as good sights many times in tarts."

The hedge maze that the tourist wanders in nowadays at Hampton Court is quite unlike that which the Tudors knew, for theirs was a dwarf maze of hyssop, lavender cotton, winter savory, thyme, or germander. In *The Profitable Art of Gardening* are two designs for dwarf mazes "that who that listeth, having such room in their garden, may place the one of them . . . for the only purpose to sport them in at times." Hill suggested that a "herber decked with roses" occupy the center, with sundry fruit trees in the corners. A hedge maze, however, is described by Lawson: "Mazes well framed, a man's height, may perhaps make your friend wander in gathering of berries till he cannot recover himself without your help." During the long winter months, the intricate knots and mazes of low-growing evergreen plants must have provided a certain amount of outdoor pleasure when nothing else bloomed.

The Elizabethan pleasure garden was full of such adornments as carved wooden beasts, topiary work, vases of lead or stone, statues, fountains, and sundials. Carved, painted, and brightly gilded heraldic lions, greyhounds, dragons, hinds, antelopes, griffins, leopards, tigers, and badgers were common not only to English gardens but also to those of France and Italy. In her garden at Whitehall, Elizabeth had thirty-four such figures, standing on wooden pedestals and holding aloft pennants of the Queen's arms. Many such figures were also set at Hampton Court. Topiary work could be found in most of the small gardens, and Lawson encouraged the gardener to "frame your lesser wood to the shape of men armed in the field ready to give battle, of swift-running greyhounds, or of well-scented and true-running hounds to chase the deer or hunt the hare. This kind of hunting shall not waste your corn nor much your coin." Yew and privet were most commonly used in topiary work, rosemary sometimes. Again, Bacon did not approve: "I, for my part, do not like images cut out in juniper or other garden stuff; they be for children." He also frowned at vases and statues in the garden: "Great princes . . . sometimes add statues and such things for state and magnificence but nothing to the true pleasure of a garden." Such decorations were placed between the flower beds, on the terrace, or along the walks, the vases either filled with flowers or simply used for ornament.

The central embellishment remained the fountain, found in both the medieval and the Elizabethan garden. Writers often referred to the fountain as a *jet d'eau*, suggesting the French origin of such contrivances. Parkinson wanted a garden with "a fountain in the midst thereof to convey water to every part of the garden, either in pipes under the ground or brought by hand and emptied into large cisterns or great Turkey jars, placed in convenient places." Bacon thought highly of fountains but denounced pools because they attracted flies and frogs. In William Brenchley Rye's *England as Seen by Foreigners* (1865), there is a description of the fountain that Frederick,

Duke of Württemberg, saw at Hampton Court in 1592: "In the middle of the first and principal court stands a splendid high and massy fountain with an ingenious waterwork, by which you can, if you like, make the water to play upon the ladies and others who are standing by and give them a thorough wetting." Other fountains graced the courtyards of Nonsuch, Whitehall, and Kenilworth; the one at Whitehall had with it a sundial.

Besides its ornamental function and occasional use for a practical joke, water served other purposes in the garden. Through the orchard at Littlecote flowed a trout stream, and in a similar stream in the Winchester deanery garden Izaak Walton used to fish; mention is made of many streams in Francis Carew's garden at Beddington in Surrey; and at Hatfield flower beds, arbors, and walks adorned the banks on one side of the stream, called the "dell," and ornamental bridges connected this bank with the vineyard on the opposite side.

The later seventeenth century brought with it a growing trend toward simplicity and a greater classical spirit in design. There was less emphasis upon fantasy such as topiary beasts, and some elements, such as summerhouses, were more tastefully designed. But the older Elizabethan garden, described in this passage from Spenser's *The Faerie Queene,* Book IV, survived to interest later generations:

> Fresh shadowes, fit to shroud from sunny ray;
> Faire lawnds, to take the sunne in season dew;
> Sweet springs, in which a thousand Nymphs did play;
> Soft rombling brookes, that gentle slomber drew;
> High reared mounts, the lands about to vew;
> Low looking dales, disloignd from common gaze;
> Delightfull bowres, to solace louers trew;
> False Labyrinthes, fond runners eyes to daze;
> All which by nature made did nature selfe amaze.
>
> And all without were walkes and alleyes dight,
> With diuers trees, enrang'd in euen rankes;

And here and there were pleasant arbors pight,
And shadie seates, and sundry flowring bankes,
To sit and rest the walkers wearie shankes.

The availability of new plants from foreign parts must have constantly refreshed the spirit of the doughty soul who enjoyed experimenting in his own garden. The daffodil, fritillary, hyacinth, crocus or saffron flower, tulip, flower-de-luce, anemone, and French cowslip or bear's ear—all common English flowers today—were classified by Parkinson as "outlandish" (i.e., foreign). Also new on English soil in the late sixteenth and early seventeenth centuries were candytufts, lilacs, sunflowers, everlastings, and Persian marigolds. Certainly the introduction of the tulip into western Europe was of major importance to the economy of Holland, and in England, Parkinson wrote, people were

more delighted in the search, curiosity, and rarities of these pleasant delights than any age, I think, before. But, indeed, this flower above many other deserveth his true commendations and acceptance with all lovers of these beauties, both for the stately aspect and for the admirable varieties of colors that daily do arise in them. . . . But above and beyond all others, the tulipas may be so matched, one coloring answering and setting off another, that the place where they stand may resemble a piece of curious needlework or piece of painting; and I have known in a garden the master as much commended for this artificial form in placing the colors of tulips as for the goodness of his flowers or any other thing. . . . But to tell you of all the sorts of tulipas (which are the pride of delight)— they are so many and, as I may say, almost infinite—doth pass my ability and, as I believe, the skill of any other. . . . Besides this glory of variety in colors that these flowers have, they carry so stately and delightful a form and do abide so long in their bravery (enduring above three whole months from the first unto the last) that there is no lady or gentlewoman of any worth that is not caught with this delight or not delighted with these flowers.

From Tusser's lists of planting dates for the housewife we can assume that a typical farmhouse garden would contain sweet Williams, sweet Johns, bachelor's-buttons, snapdragons, roses, poppies, gillyflowers, star-of-Bethlehem, star-of-Jerusalem, eglantine, hollyhocks, lilies, valerian, and columbines. The much-loved spring flowers would also be included—the cowslips, daffodils, primroses (Parkinson's "first ambassadors" of spring), and the violets (symbols of constancy).

Concurrent with this influx of new plants was another development. The English were using flowers and herbs more and more, not just for medicinal purposes but also for ornamenting their homes, for cooking, for concocting their cosmetic potions, and for strewing their chamber floors. Many folk believed in the efficacy of rosemary and sage, prescribed in *The English Housewife*, for the passions of the heart: "Take rosemary and sage, of each an handful, and seethe them in white or strong ale, and then let the patient drink it lukewarm." Nosegays adorned the bedchambers and, during the Yule season, rosemary and other greens bedecked the manor home. Flower petals were used in cooking; Markham's recipe for a preserved salad with vinegar included violets, primroses, gillyflowers, cowslips, and broom flowers. Ladies might wear a damask powder of ground rose leaves and cloves, and herbs like meadowsweet, Elizabeth's favorite, would cover the bedchamber floor.

The rose was the most important English flower, and there are probably more references to it in English literature than to any other flower. For example, Emilia in *Two Noble Kinsmen* (II.ii) comments:

Emilia.   Of all flowers,
          Methinks a rose is best.
Woman.   Why, gentle madam?
Emilia. It is the very emblem of a maid,
     For when the west wind courts her gently,
     How modestly she blows and paints the sun
     With her chaste blushes! When the north comes near her,
     Rude and impatient, then, like chastity,
     She locks her beauties in her bud again,
     And leaves him to base briers.

Lawson bragged that he produced gillyflowers as big as roses and in nine or ten different colors. Undoubtedly such results were not uncommon, for the varieties of the pink—the carnations, gillyflowers, and single and double pinks—were, according to Parkinson, "the chiefest flowers of account in all our English gardens."

This goodly great old English carnation . . . riseth up with a great, thick, round stalk, divided into several branches, somewhat thickly set with joints, and at every joint two long green rather than whitish leaves, somewhat broader than gillyflower leaves, turning or winding two or three times round. . . . The flowers stand at the tops of the stalks in long, great, and round green husks, which are divided into five points, out of which rise many long and broad pointed leaves, deeply jagged at the ends, set in order round and comely, making a gallant great double flower of a deep carnation color, almost red. . . . The red clove gillyflower . . . grow[s] like unto the carnations but not so thickset with joints and leaves; the stalks are more, the leaves are narrower and whiter for the most part. . . . The flowers are smaller, yet very thick and double in most, and the green husks wherein they stand are smaller likewise than the former. . . . The single and double pinks are for form and manner of growing in all parts like unto the gillyflowers before described, saving only that their leaves are smaller and shorter, in some more or less than in others, and so are the flowers also.

Francis Bacon longed for a perpetual spring, *ver perpetuum,* in his garden. In late November, December, and January he could then look out at the verdant hues of holly, ivy, cypress, fir, rosemary, lavender, myrtle, and germander. He would plant the crocus, primrose, early tulip, anemone, and hyacinth for late January and February; blue violet, yellow daffodil, flowering peach, and daisy for March; and the cowslip, flower-de-luce, stock gillyflower, and white violet for April. Roses, honeysuckles, French marigolds, columbines, and apples would flower in May and June, and plum trees, musk roses, and more gillyflowers would bedeck the July garden. For August, Bacon

27

desired apricots, barberries, filberts, muskmelons, and pears, and for September, pears, nectarines, grapes, poppies, and apples. This cycle would end in October and early November with roses, hollyhocks, medlars, and bullaces.

With the advent of the more formal pleasure garden, flowers and shrubs tended to displace the vegetables and medicinal herbs, and a new garden, more utilitarian, was planned at the side of the house. Even though vegetables like the potato from the New World and spinach from the Continent were newly grown in England at this time and vegetables had become more plentiful in the daily diet, particularly in salads, little evidence exists for Harrison's statement that vegetables had suffered neglect from the period of Henry IV until the last years of Henry VII's reign because they were considered "food more meet for hogs and savage beasts to feed upon than mankind."

One can determine the extent to which herbs and vegetables were grown in the early seventeenth century from Gervase Markham's instructions in *The English Housewife*. Markham felt that no matter how herbs and vegetables were used—in pot, salad, or sauce or as a garnish—the housewife should acquire from everyday experience a firsthand knowledge of them; indeed, such was the first step in learning to be a good cook. He recommended the new moon of February as the time for her to sow gourds, cresses, borage, spike, garlic, coriander, chervil, bugloss, marjoram, radishes, rosemary, white poppy, double marigolds, thyme, and purslane; the full moon for planting anise, violets, blites, skirrets, fennel, parsley, and white succory; and the old moon for seeding lettuce, cabbage, melons, parsnips, leeks, onions, diverse grains, cucumbers, green and white cole, and holy thistle. She should plant during the full March moon succory and apples of love (tomatoes), and at the wane of the moon artichokes, basil, cole cabbage, citrons, samphire, spinach, gillyflowers, mugworts, flower-gentle, and savory. All through the year asparagus, coleworts, spinach, lettuce, parsnips, radishes, and chives could be planted.

Such an ample kitchen garden would not have been unusual on the manor domain, if we can judge by the variety of ingredients necessary for this salad recipe of Markham's:

To compound an excellent salad and which, indeed, is usual at great feasts and upon princes' tables, take a good quantity of blanched almonds and with your shredding knife cut them grossly. Then take as many raisins of the sun clean washed and the stones picked out, as many figs shred like the almonds, as many capers, twice so many olives, and as many currants as of all the rest clean washed, a good handful of the small tender leaves of red sage and spinach. Mix all these well together with good store of sugar and lay them in the bottom of a great dish. Then put unto them vinegar and oil and scrape more sugar over all. Then take oranges and lemons and, paring away the outward peels, cut them into thin slices; then with those slices cover the salad all over. Which done, take the fine, thin leaf of the red coleflower [probably, red cabbage] and with them cover the oranges and lemons all over. Then over those red leaves lay another course of old olives and the slices of well-pickled cucumbers, together with the very inward heart of your cabbage lettuce, cut into slices. Then adorn the sides of the dish and the top of the salad with mo slices of lemons and oranges and so serve it up.

A sense of orderliness in the arrangement of the garden is discernible in the directions laid down in Estienne's *Maison Rustique*. Seeds should not be sown helter-skelter wherever a bit of open ground provided a spot for planting, as had sometimes been the practice in earlier gardens. The French kitchen garden described in the English translation of this book derived its charm from order. It had pleasurable effects, too, like the "turrets of lattice fashion, covered over with Bordeaux vines, or with the best sets of vines that are to be got in the country." Large plots of turnips and coleworts were set in the center of the garden. In another section were beds for spinach, beets, orach, rocket, parsley, and sorrel. The author suggests a bed of mixed salad greens—lettuce, purslane, rocket, and sorrel—seeded in a sheep's trottle (dung), to be placed eighteen inches into the ground. In this fashion the greens would "all grow up together from one and the same root." Artichokes edged these beds. Rootlike vegetables grew in another area; separate beds were planted in leeks and chives, onions and cibols, and garlic, scallions, and carrots. Paths, at least three feet wide, ran between these sections. Smaller single plots were planned for the "winter potherbs," such as sage, hyssop, thyme, marjoram, balm, basil, savory, and costmary. Estienne names other potherbs for the kitchen garden, including endive, succory, burnet, blites, borage, bugloss, tarragon, smallage, cress, asparagus, skirrets, mustard, poppy, radishes, parsnips, cucumbers, gourds, and pompions.

At the far end of the kitchen garden grew the medicinal herbs. In the physic garden might be planted valerian, milfoil, mugwort, houseleek, patience, mercury, pellitory, nicotiana, hollyhocks, gentian, celandine, elecampane, goldenrod, eyebright, silver grass, fern, crowfoot, dead nettle, adder's-tongue, periwinkle, pimpernel, centaury, angelica, fumitory, Solomon's-seal, germander, peony, and honeysuckle.

These lists are noteworthy because they indicate the predominance of herbs in the sixteenth-century kitchen garden. Almost every plant—whether vegetable or flower—possessed curative powers for either physical or mental maladies. Only a few flowers were planted for their blossoms alone; even tulips inadvertently got into the kitchen, for Parkinson asserts that many mistook these bulbs for onions and added them to their broths and pottages. This mentor of garden lore and knowledge also tells us that garden clary comforted men and women with weak backs, that sage brewed in an ale was for pregnant women in danger of miscarrying, and that pennyroyal not only cured stomach disorders and loosened lung congestions but also relaxed one's muscles while bathing. Nevertheless, holding up the vigor of bygone days as a testimony to the virtues of the herbs, Parkinson admonishes the present for its neglect of them.

The former age of our great-grandfathers had all these hot herbs in much and familiar use, both for their meats and medicines, and therewith preserved themselves in long life and much health; but this delicate age of ours, which is not pleased with anything almost, be it meat or medicine, that is not pleasant to the palate, doth wholly refuse these almost, and therefore cannot be partaker of the benefit of them.

Of the new vegetables in Elizabethan England, the potato caused the most excitement. Nevertheless, it was not until nearly two centuries after its introduction that the potato became an important staple of diet for the multitude. The sweet potato had been known in Europe since Christopher Columbus carried it back to Spain. It is the sweet potato that Shakespeare mentioned ("Let the sky rain potatoes"—*Merry Wives of Windsor* [V.v]) and that Gerard called the common potato, an appellation that has confused people ever since. The new potato, which is our common white potato today, was discovered by the Spaniards on the Pacific coast of South America about 1580. This is cited as the Virginia potato by Gerard because in 1585 or 1586 one of Sir Walter Raleigh's expeditions brought it back from that region. The plant, however, was not indigenous to Virginia; its cultivation had probably spread there sometime in the sixteenth century from Peru and the area now part of Colombia and Ecuador. Gerard describes it as being

thick, fat, and tuberous, not much differing either in shape, color, or taste from the common potatoes, saving that the roots hereof are not so great nor long, some of them round as a ball, some oval or egg fashion, some longer and others shorter; which knobby roots are fastened unto the stalks with an infinite number of thready strings.

He adds that the potato, "a meat for pleasure," be "either roasted in embers or boiled and eaten with oil, vinegar, and pepper"—cooking methods not dissimilar to ours. Roasted with marrow, sugar, and spices, cooked with fruit, or sopped in wine

—these were the several ways that the sweet potato was prepared.

And old rhyme runs

> Hops, reformation, bays, and beer
> Came into England all in one year.

The impact on English social customs of communication with Holland in the sixteenth and seventeenth centuries should never be underestimated. There existed a two-way traffic across the Channel. French Huguenots, long resident in Holland, found in England a refuge from the chaotic conditions caused by the religious wars with Spain in the Low Countries. Once settled in England, they taught the English, for instance, that asparagus and watercress had edible as well as medicinal virtues. English soldiers, who had gone out with Leicester and others to the Low Countries to succor the Protestant cause, also returned with new vegetables to grace the English table. Samuel Hartlib wrote in his *Legacy of Husbandry* (1651) that

some old men in Surrey, where it [gardening] flourisheth very much at present, report that they knew the first gardeners that came into those parts to plant cabbages, cauliflowers, and to sow turnips, carrots, and parsnips, and to sow rathe (or early ripe) rape, peas, all of which at that time were great rarities, we having few or none in England but what came from Holland and Flanders.

Hartlib adds, however, that the cultivation of these vegetables was still not widespread in the seventeenth century. Most of this gardening was in the London and Norwich areas, where large numbers of Huguenots had settled, or in Kent, where the town of Sandwich became famous for its carrots.

Many parts of England are as yet ignorant. Within these twenty years a famous town within less than twenty miles of London had not so much as a mess of peas but what came from London, where at present gardening flourisheth much. I could instance divers other places, both in the north and west of England, where the name of gardening and hoeing is scarcely known; in which places a few gardeners might have saved the lives of many poor people who have starved these dear years.

It is not incredible, then, that Henry VIII's Queen Catherine, over a hundred years earlier, obtained her salad ingredients from Holland.

Also new in the late sixteenth century was the attentive care given to the cultivation of melons. Writing of sugar melons, pear melons, and muskmelons, Parkinson says that "this country hath not had until of late years the skill to nurse them up kindly," adding that formerly they had been cultivated by noblemen's gardeners or imported from France for the royal household. "Now divers others, that have skill and conveniency of ground for them, do plant them and make them more common." Parkinson has to admit, however, that few Englishmen attained any great measure of perfection in their melon patches, probably because of the cold climate. Plat's instructions, in *The Garden of Eden*, for planting muskmelons are of interest:

Get a load or two of fresh horse dung, such as is not above eight or ten days old or not exceeding fourteen. Lay it on a heap till it have gotten a great heat and then make a bed thereof, an ell long, and half a yard broad, and eighteen inches high, in some sunny place, treading every lay down very hard as you lay it. Then lay thereon three inches thick of fine, black, sifted mold; prick in at every three or four inches' distance a muskmelon seed, which hath first been steeped twenty-four hours in milk. . . . You must watch them carefully when they first appear, for then you must give them an hour's sun in the morning and another in the afternoon.

The other popular vine-growing plants were pumpkins, or "pompions," and cucumbers. The pompions were eaten by both the city and country poor and were either baked—seeded and stuffed with pippins, "a dainty dish"—or boiled in beef broth, milk, or water and served with butter. Parkinson mentions several varieties of cucumbers: the long green, the short, the long yellow, and an early ripe cucumber called the French kind. "In many countries they use to eat cucumbers as we do apples or pears, paring and giving slices of them as we would to our friends of some dainty apple or pear." Imported pickled cucumbers were also used in meat sauces.

By the early seventeenth century there were three kinds of artichokes in England. The first, of course, was the globe artichoke, long familiar to English soil and cooked, then as now, by boiling it in water, adding a little vinegar and pepper, and serving it with butter. The vegetable was of such high quality that many were exported to Italy, France, and the Low Countries. It is the globe artichoke that William Cecil refers to in a letter to his son, Robert, written from Theobalds on June 9, 1598, shortly before he died. "As yet I cannot recover my appetite, only I supped yesternight with four or five leaves of an artichoke." The second type, the thistlelike cardoon, enjoyed little popularity, perhaps because, as Parkinson states, "we cannot yet find the true manner of dressing them that our country may take delight therein." The English first received the third kind, the Jerusalem artichoke, in 1617. Explorers had found this vegetable in its native eastern North America, and the Indians had taught them how to cultivate and prepare it, for the Jerusalem artichoke was a favored food of the redskins. Its misnomer, "potatoes of Canada," was furnished by Parkinson, for the tuberous plant does resemble a potato in composition and is so easy to grow that it is used as feed for livestock. Parkinson believed that people erroneously called these tubers artichokes because their cooked roots tasted like globe artichoke bottoms. He also mentioned that

by reason of their great increasing [the Jerusalem artichokes are] grown to be so common here with us at London that even the most vulgar begin to despise them, whereas when they were first received among us they were dainties for a queen, . . . but the too frequent use, especially being so plentiful and cheap, hath rather bred a loathing than a liking of them.

It is surprising to note the extent that saffron and skirrets were grown in the Tudor and Stuart kitchen gardens, since saffron is now a market crop and skirrets long ago disappeared from the vegetable bed. Tusser, however, urged housewives to plant a saffron patch, and Gerard wrote that the "common or the best-known saffron groweth plentifully in Cambridgeshire, Saffron Walden [in Essex], and other places thereabout, as corn in the fields." As a crop it had political implications, for when in 1549 the commoners rebelled against the landlords, who were sheep farming on the common lands, and slaughtered 20,000 sheep outside of Norfolk, another wrong to be rectified concerned the enclosure of saffron grounds. The herb was used to flavor meat, scent the linen chest, cure an ailment, or dye a piece of cloth. In *The Comedy of Errors* (IV.iv), Antipholus of Ephesus refers to the yellow color of its dye when he asks his wife Adriana

> Did this companion with the saffron face
> Revel and feast it at my house today?

Whether fried like a fritter or baked in a pie with chestnuts and hard-boiled eggs, the skirret was a popular root vegetable, described by Parkinson as "very pleasant, far beyond any parsnip, as all agree that taste them." After praising the quality of their nourishment, Gerard cautioned that "they are something windy, by reason whereof they also provoke lust."

During the reign of Elizabeth kitchen gardens also produced peas, beans, beets, spinach, onions, lettuce, cauliflowers, cabbages, radishes, turnips, mustard, and garlic. These vegetables, however, were not cultivated throughout the land nor in any prodigious amounts, for at that time great quantities of onions, cabbages, and cauliflowers were imported from the Low Countries. Even then the presence of vegetables in the customary fare of the yeoman's table was the exception rather than the rule. By the early seventeenth century, however, cauliflowers, cabbages, Brussels sprouts, spinach, and peas were more familiar and carrots and asparagus had been introduced. A great deal of relevant information about these vegetables can be gleaned from Parkinson's *Paradisi in sole*. Here the author extols the quality of English seeds and implies that the native supply cannot meet the rising domestic demand for vegetable seeds:

Although our chief gardeners do still provide their own seed of divers things from their own ground, because, as I said, it is of the best kind, yet you must understand also that good store of the same sorts of seeds are brought from beyond the seas, for that which is gathered in this land is not sufficient to serve every man's use in the whole kingdom by many parts; yet still it is true that our English seed of many things is better than any that cometh from beyond the seas, as, for example, radish, lettuce, carrots, parsnips, turnips, cabbages, and leeks, . . . for these are by them so husbanded that they do not sow their own grounds with any other seed of these sorts but their own.

Parkinson speaks of several varieties of onions, including the Spanish, "very sweet and eaten by many like an apple." He mentions the different cabbages: the ordinary cabbage, the red cabbage, the sugar-loaf cabbage, and the Savoy cabbage; but he feels that the cauliflower "hath a much pleasanter taste . . . and is therefore of the more regard and respect at good men's tables." Along with another derivative of the cabbage, the Brussels sprout, these members of the *Brassica* genus make up today a significant portion of the Englishman's diet. According to Parkinson, the Dutch taught the English the common method of cooking spinach, another new vegetable:

Stew the herb in a pot or pipkin without any other moisture than its own, and after the moisture is a little pressed from it . . . put butter and a little spice unto it and make therewith a dish that many delight to eat of. It is used likewise to be made into tarts and many other varieties of dishes.

The turnip, cultivated in the kitchen garden of the Tudors, would become in the seventeenth century an important field crop. Mustard was grown for its seeds, which were used for mustard sauce or in medicinal concoctions.

As for beans, although French and kidney beans did exist, the poor people generally ate broad beans. Parkinson lists several kinds of peas: rounceval, green hasting, sugar, spotted, gray, white hasting, peas without skins, Scottish, and French or Fulham; and he adds that peas dried and boiled into a kind of broth or pottage with herbs are "much used in town and country in the Lent time, especially of the poorer sort of people. It is much used likewise at sea for them that go long voyages and is for change, because it is fresh, a welcome diet to most persons therein." Gerard wrote that peas were "set and sown in gardens, as also in the fields, in all places of England."

The orchards of Albion served both a utilitarian and an aesthetic purpose. They were planted to provide a pleasant garden space near the house where one could walk in the cool of the evening. According to Lawson, writing in 1618, the orchard was "the honest delight of one wearied with the works of his lawful calling." Lawson's enthusiasm is contagious: "The very works of and in an orchard and garden are better than the ease and rest of and from other labors. . . . What was Paradise but a garden and orchard of trees and herbs, full of pleasure and nothing there but delights?"

Because the orchard had a purpose higher than mere fruit production, the Englishman planned it for artistic effects. Fruit trees were to be planted, Gervase Markham writes in *The English Husbandman,* in rows so that "which way soever a man shall cast his eyes yet he shall see the trees every way stand on rows, making squares, alleys, and divisions according to a man's imagination." A fountain or a small banqueting house might grace the center of Markham's orchard, since his country estate would be larger than Lawson's. As mentioned earlier, in the small country homes the orchard and the pleasure garden were very likely one and the same, with flowers and herbs, like saffron and licorice, planted between the trees, with seats banked by camomile, and with sanded paths and tree-shaded alleys for walking. In the larger gardens, where a gate opened from the flower garden in front of the house to the orchard at the side, the position of the orchard was generally on the northeast side: "It standeth north-northeast . . . of thy curious-knotted garden" *(Love's Labor Lost* [I.i.]) Parkinson gives logical reasons for this placement of the orchard:

First, for that the fruit trees, being grown great and tall, will be a great shelter from the north and east winds, which may offend your chiefest garden, and although that your orchard stand a little bleak upon the winds, yet trees rather endure these strong bitter blasts than other smaller and more tender shrubs and herbs can do. Secondly, if your orchard should stand behind your garden of flowers more southward, it would shadow too much of the garden and, besides, would so bind in the north and east and north and west winds upon the garden that it would spoil many tender things therein and so much abate the edge of your pleasure thereof that you would willingly wish to have no orchard rather than that it should so much annoy you by the so ill standing thereof. Thirdly, the falling leaves, being still blown with the wind so abundantly into the garden, would either spoil many things or have one daily and continual attending thereon to cleanse and sweep them away.

Parkinson further urged that walnut, elm, ash, or oak trees be planted a distance from the orchard in order to protect the fruit trees against "high, boisterous, and cold winds."

The Tudors and Stuarts did not want for fruit, nuts, and berries. By the turn of the sixteenth century apricots, almonds, gooseberries, raspberries, currants, melons (discussed earlier), oranges, lemons, and cornelian cherries had been introduced to a country which for some time had grown an imposing array of apples, pears, plums, nectarines, damsons, medlars, quinces, figs, pomegranates, cherries, peaches, walnuts, hazelnuts, filberts, chestnuts, strawberries, mulberries, blackberries, dewberries, bilberries (or whortleberries, the European blueberries), barberries, and grapes. According to Harrison, "the orchards were never furnished with so good fruit nor with such variety as at this present." Fruit was extremely popular and there are many literary references to it—witness Titania's speech in *Midsummer Night's Dream* (III.i):

> Feed him with apricots and dewberries,
> With purple grapes, green figs, and mulberries.

And there are many more. The following jingle from Tusser concerns the farmer's tasks for the month of December:

> Good fruit and good plenty doth well in thy loft;
> Then make thee an orchard and cherish it oft.
> For plant or for stock lay aforehand to cast,
> But set or remove it ere Christmas be past.

Fencing such a stock of fruit cost a great deal, since the orchard naturally extended over an area larger than the other gardens required. Most farmers erected mud walls or, preferably, planted quickset hedges. Parkinson, however, advised those who could afford the expense to build brick or stone walls; "the gaining of ground and profit of the fruit trees planted thereagainst will in short time recompense that charge." An eye was also given to the form of the orchard. Parkinson desired a broad path laid between the wall and the orchard "that the wall shall not be hindered of the sun but have sufficient comfort for your trees, . . . the distance between them and the wall being a sufficient space for their shadow to fall into." He would then encompass the fruit trees with a low hedge of cornelian cherry trees and rose, gooseberry, and currant bushes. In this fashion the walk would be enclosed and "both it and your orchard in better form and manner than if it lay open." A similar plan was considered by Lawson: several round knots or a maze of berry bushes, leaving ample space for a path, "for it is to be noted that the eye must be pleased with the form." Parkinson advised that the walls lying "open to the south and southwest sun are fittest to be planted with your tenderest and earliest fruits, as apricots, peaches, nectarines, and May or early cherries; the east, north, and west, for plums and quinces." Lawson deplored the common seventeenth-century practice of training fruit trees along the walls with tacks and other means. Care was taken to plant the trees far enough apart so that at full growth their branches would not bruise one another but would gently interlace to form arches. According to Parkinson, the damson, bullace, and tall plum were to be planted on the outside and the low plum, cherry, and apple on the inside, with the pear behind or beside the lower trees, affording it shelter from the north and east sides. "Other sorts of fruit trees you may mix among these if you please, as filberts, cornelian cherries in standards, and medlars." In the north country of his native Yorkshire, Lawson advised against trying to grow apricots, peaches, and quinces.

Besides the fact that the apricot did not flourish in Yorkshire, some rural areas probably were not as yet familiar with the fruit, which had been introduced in the early sixteenth century. Parkinson mentions different apricots: the great or long, the small round, the white, the masculine, the long masculine, and the Algerian, which John Tradescant, the famous seventeenth-century plant collector and onetime gardener to Charles I, had found while fighting pirates on the Algerian coast in 1620. The apricot, of course, was believed to have medicinal properties. Parkinson states that the oil from the fruit's kernel assuaged inflamed hemorrhoids, ulcers, and earaches. In advising a fertilizer for apricot trees, Sir Hugh Plat added to the mundane combination of well-rotted cow and horse dung, mixed with earth, the surprising ingredient claret!

Citrus trees were first grown in England at this time. In *The Natural History and Antiquities of the County of Surrey* (1718–1719), the seventeenth-century antiquary John Aubrey describes an orangery at Beddington, the Carew family estate in Surrey,

where are several orange trees . . . planted in the open ground, where they have throve to admiration for above a century but are preserved during the winter season under a movable covert. They were brought from Italy by Sir Francis Carew . . . and it was the first attempt of this kind that we hear of.

Apparently Carew also imported trees from France, for in 1562 William Cecil wrote to Thomas Windebank (in whose care his son Thomas was entrusted during a stay in Paris), requesting a lemon tree:

I have already an orange tree, and if the price be not much I pray you procure for me a lemon, a pomegranate, and a myrt tree and help that they may be sent home to London with Mr. Carew's trees; and beforehand send me in writing a perfect declaration how they ought to be used, kept, and ordered.

Windebank complied, purchasing a lemon tree for fifteen crowns, the cheapest to be had, and answered that "My Lord Ambassador and Mr. Carew were the choosers of it" (quoted by Alicia Amherst, *A History of Gardening in England* [London, 1896]). The fact that the Queen's most trusted counselor possessed only one lemon tree and one orange tree indicates their novelty. The miserable English climate was hardly suitable for rearing citrus fruit. Parkinson wanted to move orange trees to a closed gallery during the cold months, since "no tent or mean provision will preserve them." One compensation for all this trouble was mentioned by Gerard, who claimed that a brew of sliced oranges and mercury sublimate in boiling water would relieve a person's itch or manginess.

The English countryside yielded such an abundance of apples, pears, and cherries in the sixteenth and seventeenth centuries that after setting aside enough fruit for the family's consumption the yeoman generally had a surplus to sell. The farmers of Kent, Norfolk, Sussex, and Surrey could vend their fruit in the ready markets of nearby London.

Apples came in many varieties: the Davy gentle, the Master William, the summer and russet pippins, the pomewater, the flower of Kent, the gillyflower, the Kentish codling, the pound royal, the leathercoat, and the spicing, to cite a few. When the clown said, "I must have saffron to color the warden pies," in *The Winter's Tale* (IV.iii), he was referring to a pie made of pears. Other popular pears were the bon crétien, the Windsor, and the bergamot. Worcestershire grew as famous for pears as Kent did for cherries.

Elizabethans had a belief that a plant adopted the qualities of its neighbors. The strawberry, however, was an exception; it remained pure strawberry in character. According to Parkinson, "the wild strawberry that groweth in the woods is our garden strawberry, but better by the soil and transplanting." The fruit was generally served with claret or cream and sugar.

Wine culture, common during and before Elizabeth's day, became nearly nonexistent as time wore on. In the Middle Ages vineyards had been associated with the monasteries, and those at Ely had attained fame. Plat charges the disappearance of vineyards to ignorance. Parkinson is more kind: "The wine of late made hath been but small and not durable, like that which cometh from beyond sea, whether our unkindly years or the want of skill or a convenient place for a vineyard be the cause I cannot well tell you."

Orchards frequently included mulberry trees, which provided fruit as well as leaves on which silkworms fed. During the reign of James I a mania for silk production swept England, and the King himself wrote an introduction to a treatise on the subject and ordered mulberry trees planted in every county town. Near Westminster Palace he had his own orchard of mulberry trees. In 1607 a French treatise, *The Perfect Use of Silkworms,* by Olivier de Serres, was translated and published. Concurrently, the Virginia Company of London was trying to establish both silk and wine production in Virginia. A century later Englishmen were persuaded to emigrate to Georgia to furnish labor for silk production. For the same reason French Huguenots, skilled in the culture of silk, were urged to settle in South Carolina. There some silk was produced, but expensive labor hindered any large-scale activity.

The serious fruiterer harvested with caution, taking care when and how to pick his fruit. Lawson said,

Gather at the full of the moon for keeping; gather dry for fear of rotting. Gather the stalks withal, for a little wound in fruit is deadly; but not the stump that must bear the next fruit, nor leaves, for moisture putrifies. Gather every kind severally by itself, for all will not keep alike and it is hard to discern them when they are mingled.

A long ladder, a stool ladder, a gathering apron, and a "hook to pull boughs to you" were the necessary tools. The author of *The Husbandman's Fruitful Orchard* advised that only fruit that had ripened prior to falling should be gathered from the ground. Ripe fallings could be baked or roasted, but immature fruit would wither before it was fit for use.

The orchard owner had to know the art of grafting, a skill described by many of the garden writers, including Lawson:

Now we are come to the most curious point of our faculty, . . . which we commonly call "graffing" or (after some) "grafting." I cannot etymologize nor show the original of the word, but the thing is the reforming of the fruit of one tree with the fruit of another by an artificial transplacing or transposing of a twig, bud, or leaf (commonly called a "graft") taken from one tree of the same or some other kinds and placed or put to or into another tree in one time and manner. Of this there be divers kinds, but three or four now especially in use, to wit, grafting, incising, packing on, grafting in the scutcheon or inoculating; whereof the chief and most usual is called "grafting."

To Lawson, the labor that a garden required was amply rewarding, and he conveys to the reader of his book this sense of delight and satisfaction. The reader can enjoy with him the taste of ripe cherries, the smell of sweet woodbine and violets, and, particularly, the sound of bees humming and nightingales singing in the orchard:

Nay, it is no doubt a comfort to them to set open their casements into a most delicate garden and orchard, whereby they may not only see that wherein they are so much delighted but also to give fresh, sweet, and pleasant air to their galleries and chambers. . . . What can your eye desire to see, your ears to hear, your mouth to taste, or your nose to smell, that is not to be had in an orchard with abundance and variety? What more delightsome than an infinite variety of sweet-smelling flowers, decking with sundry colors the green mantle of the earth, the universal mother of us all, so by them bespotted, so dyed, that all the world cannot sample them; and wherein it is more fit to admire the Dyer than imitate His workmanship, coloring not only the earth but decking the air and sweetening every breath and spirit. . . . And all these by the skill of your gardener so comely and orderly placed in your borders and squares and so intermingled that none looking thereon cannot but wonder to see what nature corrected by art can do.

Some of the new enthusiasm for the art of gardening undoubtedly was stimulated by the example of the great personalities of the time who devoted much attention to the development of their grounds. What great men do when they put aside matters of state for recreation may influence lesser folk; the fact that men like William Cecil, Walter Raleigh, Francis Carew, and Francis Bacon were laying out grandiose gardens and importing plants for them was well known, and many followed their examples. Although Elizabeth did little directly, indirectly she encouraged the gardening of the period. She urged her noblemen to build country homes, and her progresses to such show places as Kenilworth, Wilton, and Theobalds furthered the desire of her hosts to display a beautiful garden to their sovereign. Many features of these gardens derived from Italian designs such as Henry VIII had incorporated in the gardens of Nonsuch Palace. Nonsuch was begun in 1538, and apparently the gardens, as well as the fairy-tale building, were modeled after those of the Italianate Palace of Fontainebleau, built for Francis I after his imprisonment in 1525. At Nonsuch the gardens assumed a classical unity in the placement of the flower beds, terraces, statues, fountains, and vases. The first known banqueting house in a garden was at Nonsuch. John Gerard was in charge of the gardens at Theobalds, one of the residences of William Cecil. James I, who had grown fond of Theobalds, persuaded Robert Cecil in 1607 to give it to him in exchange for Hatfield. Cecil's nephew, Francis Bacon, lived near by, and Bacon possibly had Theobalds in mind when he wrote his essay on gardens. There were many embellishments at Theobalds. Marble statues of the twelve Roman emperors stood in the summerhouse, and an extensive water garden enabled one to row a boat between the groves of fruit trees. Bacon, however, would not have approved of his uncle's statues. Some of the other great gardens were as sumptuous. Kenilworth in Warwickshire possessed an aviary and obelisks made out of red porphyry. The Earl of Pembroke's garden at Wilton had a river spanned by an ornamental bridge. The mount at Hampton Court was crowned by a banqueting house three stories high. Heraldic beasts of stone stood along the path to the top. The walls of the garden house at Beddington, Carew's home, were emblazoned with scenes showing the defeat of the Armada. Holdenby in Northamptonshire and Hardwick in Derbyshire adopted two ideas popular with us today, for their living areas stretched along an axis and glassed walls overlooked the garden.

Few vestiges of these ostentatious structures and their gardens exist today. A few gardens, open to the public, have been laid out to represent faithfully some of the Elizabethan devices. There are knot gardens at Hampton Court, Kensington Palace, and New Place in Stratford-upon-Avon, where bloom the flowers that Shakespeare alludes to in his plays. At Shakespeare's birthplace may be seen some of the fruit trees mentioned by him: the mulberry, quince, pear, apple, cherry, and medlar. The formal garden at Kensington Palace is bordered at one end by a pleached alley, and the maze at Hampton Court delights its visitors just as similar ones must have done four centuries ago.

The old-fashioned English flowers of the Tudor and Stuart period have never ceased to bloom, even when the garden acquired new forms as the centuries passed. The love of gardening born and nourished under the Elizabethans became a vital part of English character. It was natural that this feeling should be transmitted by the colonists to the New World, and that plantation owners, like William Byrd I of Westover in Virginia, should lay out gardens and import plants, seeds, and bulbs to beautify them. Because of the climate, most of the great gardens after the English manner were to be found in the southern colonies. In the South, particularly in Virginia, the rising aristocracy was attempting to emulate the life of the English country gentleman. The love of flowers is a persistent trait in the national heritage of the English-speaking people, and the development of gardening owes much to the special enthusiasm for it during one of the most glorious periods in English history.

SUGGESTED READING

Several excellent accounts of late-sixteenth- and early-seventeenth-century England by contemporary writers have been reprinted. William Harrison's *Description of England,* first printed in Raphael Holinshed's *Chronicles* (1577), is available under the title *Elizabethan England,* edited by Lothrop Withington (London, 1902). In it is included the chapter "Of Gardens and Orchards," which first appeared in the 1587 edition of Holinshed. Valuable for its picture of London and suburbs is John Stow's *Survey of London* (1598 *et seq.*), the 1603 edition of which has been edited by Charles Kingsford (2 vols., London, 1908). Material on the rural towns and countryside may be found in *The Itinerary of John Leland,* edited by Lucy Toulmin Smith (5 vols., London, 1907–1910). William Brenchley Rye, *England as Seen by Foreigners* (London, 1865) is interesting for its eyewitness accounts by foreigners traveling in England.

Useful general information will be found in Muriel St. C. Byrne, *Elizabethan Life in Town and Country* (London, 1925; rev. ed., 1954). Flemish influence on English life during this period is the subject of an informative article by John J. Murray, "The Cultural Impact of the Flemish Low Countries on Sixteenth- and Seventeenth-Century England," *American Historical Review,* LXII (July, 1957), 837–854.

The most concise survey of gardening during Shakespeare's time can be found in an essay, "Agriculture and Gardening," by R. E. Prothero (Baron Ernle), in Volume I of *Shakespeare's England* (2 vols., Oxford, 1917). The author cites passages where Shakespeare refers to garden design, flowers, fruits, and vegetables. Bacon's famous essay on gardens is printed in *The Essays of Francis Bacon,* edited by Mary Augusta Scott (New York, 1908). The editor's footnotes are very helpful.

Henry N. Ellacombe's *The Plant-Lore and Garden-Craft of Shakespeare* (London and New York, 1896) is a useful reference volume. He cites all the passages in which a plant is referred to by Shakespeare and provides much historical and botanical information on the individual plants.

The best works on the history of English gardening are Eleanour Sinclair Rohde, *The Story of the Garden* (London, 1932; 1933), and Alicia Amherst, *A History of Gardening in England* (London, 1896; 1910). Both books are well illustrated, contain bibliographies of the old garden books, and have excellent chapters on gardening in Tudor and Stuart England. Miles Hadfield, *Gardening in Britain* (London, 1960) is informative and has good descriptions of the great gardens of this period.

Eleanour Sinclair Rohde has written two books on garden literature. She treats the works of authors such as Thomas Hill, William Lawson, Gervase Markham, and John Parkinson in *The Old English Gardening Books* (London, 1924). *The Old English Herbals* (London, 1922) is concerned with the early herbalists, their botanical classifications, and their influence on plant cultivation.

Some information on flower gardens, orchards, and kitchen gardens of rural England can be found in books on farming. M. E. Seebohm, in *The Evolution of the English Farm* (London, 1927), devotes two chapters to the sixteenth and seventeenth centuries. Also good is Baron Ernle, *English Farming Past and Present* (London, 1912; 1932).

A few of the old gardening books have been reprinted. Eleanour Sinclair Rohde wrote the introduction for William Lawson, *A New Orchard and Garden* (London, 1927). Also reprinted is Sir Hugh Plat, *Delights for Ladies*, with an introduction by G. E. and Kathleen Rosemary Fussel (London, 1948). Thomas Hill, *A Most Brief and Pleasant Treatise* has been reprinted under the title *First Garden Book*, edited by Violet and Hal W. Trovillion (Herrin, Illinois, 1946).

There are numerous books on the great houses of England. Two recently published works of this sort are of particular interest: John Dent, *The Quest for Nonsuch* (London, 1962), which narrates Mr. Dent's search for the actual site of the famous palace that was demolished in the seventeenth century and gives a variety of details concerning its architecture and the amenities of life provided for its occupants; and Ian Dunlop, *Palaces and Progresses of Elizabeth I* (London, 1962), an illustrated description of such great houses and royal residences as Greenwich, Whitehall, Hampton Court, Nonsuch, Kenilworth, and Theobalds.

PLATES

Plate 1. The title page of John Gerard's *Herbal* (1597).

Plate 2. Engraved portrait of John Parkinson. Frontispiece of Parkinson's *Paradisi in sole, Paradisus terrestris* (1629).

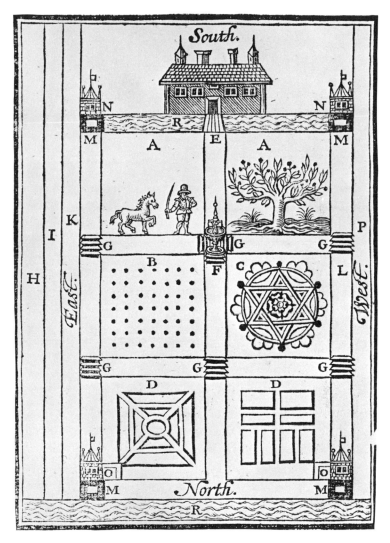

Plate 3. William Lawson's diagram for a small country estate. From *A New Orchard and Garden* (1618). See pp. 17–18.

Plate 4. Preparing beds for planting. *(Upper)* From Thomas Hill, *The Gardener's Labyrinth* (1652); *(lower)* from the 1577 edition of the same work.

Plate 5. *(Upper)* Planting in raised beds. *(Lower)* Dressing an arbor. From Thomas Hill, *The Gardener's Labyrinth* (1577).

Plate 6. (Left) A small formal garden. From Thomas Hill, *The Gardener's Labyrinth* (1577). *(Right)* Diagram of a "plain square." The author recommends placing "in the center of every square, that is to say, where the four corners of the four quarters do, as it were, neighbor and meet, either a conduit [fountain] of antic [grotesque] fashion, a standard of some unusual device, or else some dial or other pyramid that may grace and beautify the garden." From Gervase Markham, *The English Husbandman* (1613).

Plate 7. Irrigating a garden of raised beds by means of a pump and wooden troughs. From Thomas Hill, *The Gardener's Labyrinth* (1577).

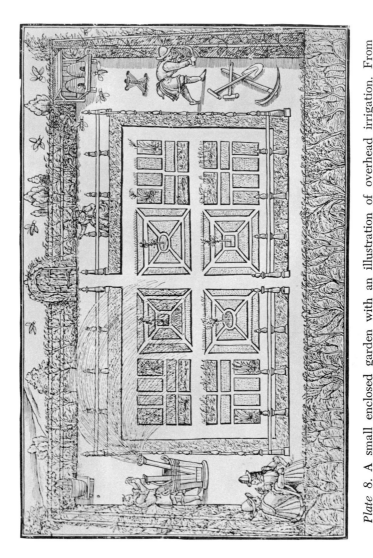

Plate 8. A small enclosed garden with an illustration of overhead irrigation. From Thomas Hill, *The Gardener's Labyrinth* (1577).

Plate 9. Dining in the garden. From Thomas Hill,
The Gardener's Labyrinth (1577).

Plate 10. A formal garden. A group dining in a pleached arbor is discernible in the upper right-hand corner. From Crispin van de Passe, *Stirpium, insignium nobilitatis* (Basle, ca. 1602).

Plate 11. A Continental garden. This view shows the new interest in exotic tropical plants. From Theodor de Bry, *Florilegium novum* (Oppenheim, 1612).

Plate 12. A Dutch enclosed garden, showing elaboration of design and topiary work. From Crispin van de Passe, *Hortus floridus* (Utrecht, ca. 1614; 1949 reprint).

Plate 13. A Dutch garden with an arbored alley and beehives. From Jacob Cats, *Monita amoris virginei* (Amsterdam, 1622).

Plate 14. Designs for *jets d'eau*. From Jan van der Groen, *Le jardinier du Pays-Bas* (Brussels, 1672).

A Maze.

Another Maze.

Plate 15. A maze. From Thomas Hill,
The Gardener's Labyrinth (1577).

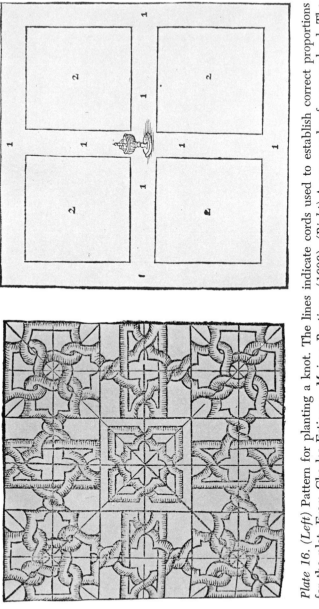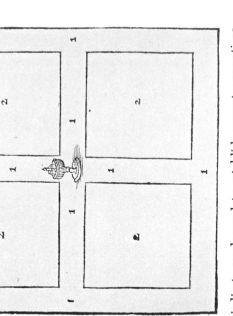

Plate 16. (*Left*) Pattern for planting a knot. The lines indicate cords used to establish correct proportions for the plot. From Charles Estienne, *Maison Rustique* (1606). (*Right*) A square plan for an orchard. The figures *1* indicate the alleys around and through the plot, and *2* designates the four quarters where fruit trees are to be planted. From Gervase Markham, *The English Husbandman* (1613).

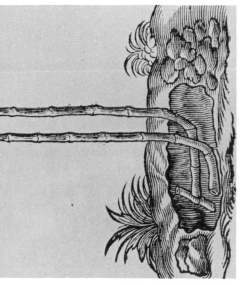

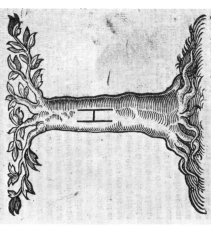

Plate 17. (Left) Figure illustrating method of grafting. Markham advises the husbandman to make a long slit, then slip the graft under the bark "flat unto the sap of the tree." The bark should then be bound down close to the graft with "a little untwound hemp or a soft woolen list [strip of fabric]." *(Above)* Vine sets should be set "in the earth slopewise, at least a foot deep, raising out of the earth, uncovered, not above four or five joints, . . . then cover them with good earth firmly, closely, and strongly." From Gervase Markham, *The English Husbandman* (1613).

When goe to the body, arme, or branch of that tree which you intend to graft, which is to be preſupposed must euer haue a ſmooth and tender barke, and with a very ſharpe knife ſlit the barke, ſtwo ſlits at leaſt, two inches long a péere, and about halfe an inch or more diſtance betwéene the ſtwo ſlits: then make another ſlit croſſe-wiſe ouer, thwart, from long ſlit to long ſlit, the figure whereof will be thus:

Then with your knife raiſe the barke gently from the trée,

Plate 18. Gathering fruit. From T. F., *A Book of Divers Devices* (1585–1622). Folger MS. V.a.311.

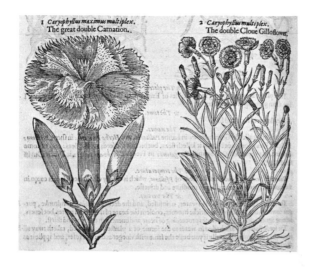

1 *Caryophyllus maximus multiplex.*
The great double Carnation.

2 *Caryophyllus multiplex.*
The double Cloue Gilloflower.

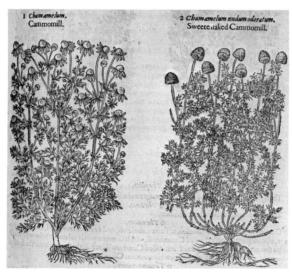

1 *Chamæmelum.*
Cammomill.

2 *Chamæmelum nudum odoratum.*
Sweete naked Cammomill.

late 19. (Upper) Carnations. *(Lower)* Camomile. Gerard recommends
amomile as good against colic and stone. It also eases chest pain,
nd "the oil compounded of the flowers . . . is a remedy against
vearisomeness." Camomile was often used for turf and paths be-
ause it was proverbially known that "the camomile, the more it is
rodden on the faster it grows." From John Gerard, *Herbal* (1597).

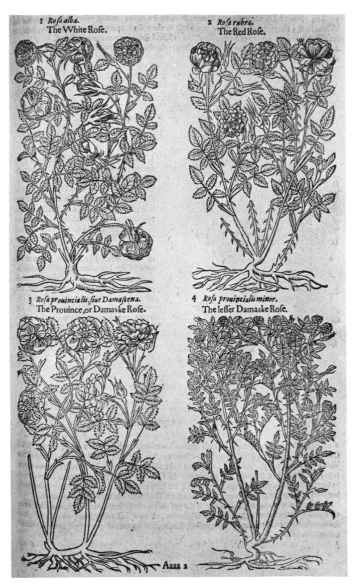

Plate 20. Varieties of roses, a flower highly favored by the Elizabethans. From John Gerard, *Herbal* (1597).